DINOSAUR FACT FRENZY!

by Mathew J. Wedel

Published by Capstone Press, an imprint of Capstone
1710 Roe Crest Drive, North Mankato, Minnesota 56003
capstonepub.com

Dinosaur Fact Frenzy! was originally published as *Totally Amazing Facts About Dinosaurs,* copyright 2018 by Capstone Press.

Copyright © 2026 by Capstone. All rights reserved. No part of this publication may be reproduced in whole or in part, or stored in a retrieval system, or transmitted in any form or by any means, electronic, mechanical, photocopying, recording, or otherwise, without written permission of the publisher.

Library of Congress Cataloging-in-Publication Data is available on the Library of Congress website.

ISBN: 9798875233524 (hardcover)
ISBN: 9798875233470 (paperback)
ISBN: 9798875233487 (ebook PDF)

Summary: There's a DINOSAUR FACT FRENZY headed your way! Did you know that Velociraptors were about the same size as a turkey? Or that Suuwassea had teeth shaped like pencils? Dozens of bite-size facts are paired with fun dinosaur images, welcoming kids to browse or to devour the book from cover to cover. Even a dedicated dino fan is sure to learn something surprising as they flip through these pages!

Editorial Credits
Editors: Alison Deering and Christianne Jones; Designer: Tracy Davies; Media Researcher: Svetlana Zhurkin; Production Specialist: Whitney Schaefer

Image Credits
Capstone: Jon Hughes, 5 (bottom), 10, 12, 13, 15 (top), 18, 20, 25 (bottom), 30, 31, 32 (top), 33, 39, 54 (top), 55 (top), 60, 61, 62, 63; Getty Images: MR1805, 53, Science Photo Library/Elabarts/Elena Hartley, 26, Science Photo Library/Roger Harris, 44, Stocktrek Images/Corey Ford, 14 (top), Stocktrek Images/Elena Duvernay, 52, Stocktrek Images/Mohamad Haghani, 11 (middle), 42 (top), Stocktrek Images/Nobumichi Tamura, 1 (left), 19 (top left), 21 (top), 27 (top), Stocktrek Images/Robert Fabiani, 22; Shutterstock: Aayam 4D, 43 (bottom), Adwo, 9, Alberto Andrei Rosu, 34, angin hiqaru87, 27 (bottom), Anton_Ivanov, 43 (top), Arthit Premprayot, 15 (bottom), Catmando, 56, CkyBe (speech bubbles), cover and throughout, Daniel Eskridge, 28, 41, Danny Ye, 58, David Herraez Calzada, cover (top left), DM7, cover (T-rex), 4 (right), Dotted Yeti, cover (middle right), 1 (right), 4 (middle), 16, 24 (top), 50 (top), 51, Ev_Parasochka, 14 (bottom), gn8 (rays and lines), cover and throughout, GolF2532, 55 (bottom), grey_and, 45 (bottom), Herschel Hoffmeyer, 49, Holiday.Photo.Top, cover (party hat), iconation, 23 (left), Ignacio Guevara, 54 (bottom), IGORdeyka, 24 (bottom), imonasaftas, 32 (bottom), JeremyWhat, 19 (top right), kamomeen, cover (top right), Mark Brandon, cover (fossil), Matthew Dicker, 57, mayu85, cover (necklace), mentalmind, 21 (medal), metha1819, 5 (top), michal812, 19 (bottom), Mr. Beekeeper, 29 (bottom), New Africa, 17 (top), Olga Yaroshenko, 59, (bottom), Oliver Denker, 36, Orla, 35, 47, rodos studio Ferhat Cinar, 6, 40, Sebastian Kaulitzki, back cover, 29 (top), 37, 38, 59 (top), Smix Ryo (dinosaur silhouettes), 3 and throughout, Stocktrek Images, 8, SvgOcean (dinosaur footprints), cover and throughout, Tsekhmister, 42 (bottom), 50 (bottom), Uglegorets, 11 (top), 25 (top), v_kulieva (gradient background), back cover and throughout, Vac1, 4 (left), Vector Tradition, cover and throughout (dinosaur skeletons), 17 (bottom), Warpaint, 46, 48, 64, William Cushman, 45 (top), YuRi Photolife, cover (bottom left), Yury Gubin, 23 (right)

Printed and bound in the USA. PO 6307

Dig into Dozens of Dinosaur Facts 4

Try-Out Triassic Period 6

Giant Jurassic Period 22

Climactic Cretaceous Period 40

DIG INTO DOZENS OF DINOSAUR FACTS

Do you love dinosaurs? Like, really, *really* love dinosaurs? Enough to know which dinosaur was the first one ever discovered? Or how about which dinosaur had teeth shaped like pencils? Or which one weighed as much as five African elephants? Even if you know *all* of that, you can still discover a frenzy of other fascinating dinosaur facts. All you have to do is turn the page!

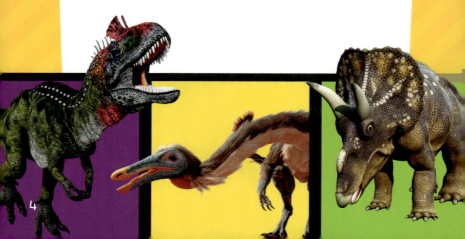

WARNING: DINO-MITE DINO FACTS AHEAD!

TRY-OUT TRIASSIC PERIOD

Dinosaurs first appeared in the Triassic Period. They tried lots of new things, including long necks and armor for the plant eaters and big heads and big teeth for the meat eaters.

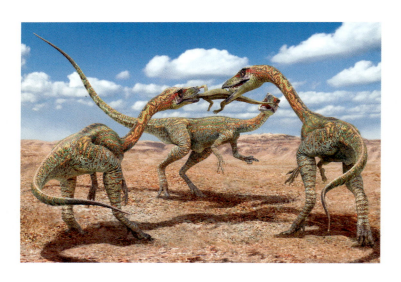

COELOPHYSIS (seel-OH-fie-sis)

These dinos lived in present-day New Mexico and Arizona in the United States and also in present-day South Africa.

WOW!

More than 1,000 Coelphysis skeletons were found in a single quarry at Ghost Ranch, New Mexico.

EORAPTOR (EE-oh-RAP-tor)

Eoraptor would grow to be a little more than 3 feet (1 meter) long.

Eoraptor had hollow bones. This made it lightweight and speedy.

HERRERASAURUS (herr-ray-rah-SORE-us)

Herrerasaurus walked on two legs as it hunted.

These dinosaurs lived in what is now Argentina.

WOW!

Herrerasaurus had five toes on each foot, but only three reached the ground.

LILIENSTERNUS (LIL-ee-en-STUR-us)

Liliensternus was close to 10 feet (3 m) long.

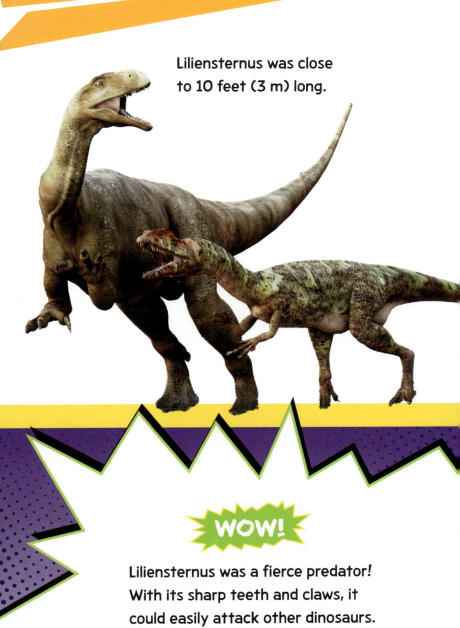

WOW!

Liliensternus was a fierce predator! With its sharp teeth and claws, it could easily attack other dinosaurs.

Sauroposeidon (SORE-oh-puh-SIGH-dun)

These dinosaurs lived in what is now Oklahoma (United States).

A Sauroposeidon's neck was more than 40 feet (12 m) long!

WOW!

Like birds, Sauroposeidon's neck bones were filled with air.

PLATEOSAURUS (PLAT-ee-oh-SORE-us)

Plateosaurus was 23 to 30 feet (7 to 9 m) long.

WOW!

Plateosaurus was a giant! It weighed up to 4 tons (3,629 kilograms).

Sometimes whole herds of these heavy dinosaurs would get trapped in mud.

Their skeletons would be preserved and were later discovered.

SATURNALIA (sat-urn-AHL-ee-ah)

Like a modern iguana, Saturnalia ate plants using its leaf-shaped teeth.

Saturnalia had a long tail that it used to turn quickly when running.

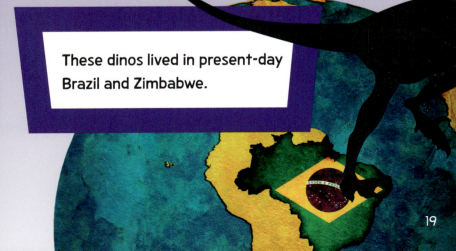

These dinos lived in present-day Brazil and Zimbabwe.

THECODONTOSAURUS
(THEEK-oh-DON-toh-SORE-us)

Thecodontosaurus was one of the earliest long-necked dinosaurs to exist on Earth.

It was also one of the first dinosaurs to be discovered.

Thecodontosaurus measured 7 feet (2 m) long.

In 1836, it became the fifth dinosaur ever to be named.

GIANT JURASSIC PERIOD

Dinosaurs spread all over the world in the Jurassic Period. They grew to enormous sizes and kept trying lots of new things. Feathered dinosaurs and the first birds were especially successful.

ALLOSAURUS (AL-oh-sore-us)

Allosaurus was 39 feet (12 m) long.

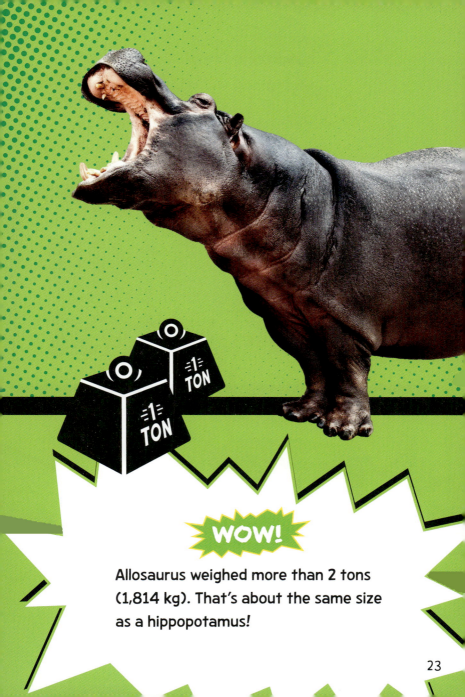

WOW!

Allosaurus weighed more than 2 tons (1,814 kg). That's about the same size as a hippopotamus!

COMPSOGNATHUS
(komp-sog-NAY-thus)

Compsognathus was a fast runner.

WOW!

Compsognathus hunted lizards and bugs. One fossil had the skeleton of a lizard in its stomach.

These dinos lived in present-day Germany and France.

25

GUANLONG (GWAN-long)

Guanlong was almost 10 feet (3 m) long.

WOW!

Guanlong caused quite a "flap" when it was discovered. It was one of the first dinosaurs found with feathers.

APATOSAURUS (ah-PAT-oh-SORE-us)

Apatosaurus was 69 feet (21 m) long.

Apatosaurus weighed about 35 tons (31,752 kg). That's the weight of about five African elephants!

TUOJIANGOSAURUS
(too-oh-jian-GO-sore-us)

Tuojiangosaurus had narrow back plates and sharp shoulder spikes.

Much like a modern porcupine, Tuojiangosaurus scared off predators with its spikes.

These dinos lived in present-day China.

SUUWASSEA (soo-wah-SEE-uh)

Suuwassea was 50 feet (15 m) long.

Suuwassea had teeth that were shaped like pencils.

This dinosaur used its teeth to strip branches of their leaves.

BRACHIOSAURUS (BRAK-ee-oh-SORE-us)

Brachiosaurus was 98 feet (30 m) long.

WOW!

Brachiosaurus was 45 feet (14 m) tall. That's more than four stories high!

Long front legs helped Brachiosaurus eat leaves from tall trees.

CRYOLOPHOSAURUS
(CRY-o-LOAF-oh-SORE-us)

Cryolophosaurus was 20 feet (6 m) long.

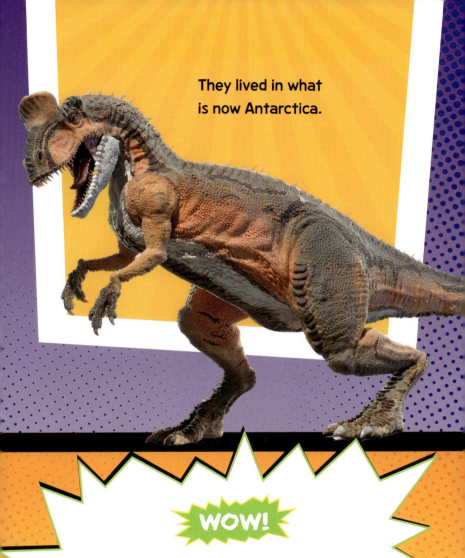

They lived in what is now Antarctica.

WOW!

It looks like this dinosaur has a fancy hairstyle, but it's a sideways crest on top of its head.

STEGOSAURUS (STEG-uh-sore-us)

Stegosaurus was 25 feet (8 m) long.

This dino had large plates pointing out of its back.

WOW!

The sharp spikes on Stegosaurus's tail could be used for defense. It could smack other dinosaurs with its tail.

CLIMACTIC CRETACEOUS PERIOD

Dinosaurs reached the peak of their success in the Cretaceous Period. The largest, most heavily armored, and most fearsome dinos ruled the earth until their extinction.

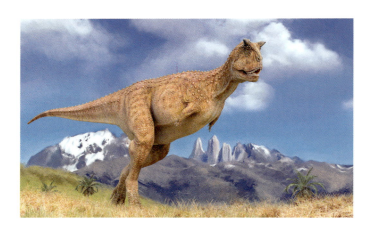

CARNOTAURUS (Kar-noh-TORE-us)

Carnotaurus was found in present-day Argentina.

Carnotaurus is named "MEAT BULL" for the horns over its eyes.

WOW!

This scaled predator was one of the fastest runners of its time.

VELOCIRAPTOR (vuh-LOS-uh-rap-ter)

Velociraptors lived in what is now Asia.

They were about the size of modern turkeys.

These dinos became popular after being featured in the *Jurassic Park* movies.

GIGANOTOSAURUS (gig-an-OH-toe-SORE-us)

Giganotosaurus was 41 feet (12.5 m) long.

Its skull was 5 feet (1.5 m) long.

WOW!

But its brain was only the size of a banana.

TYRANNOSAURUS REX
(tie-RAN-oh-SORE-us REX)

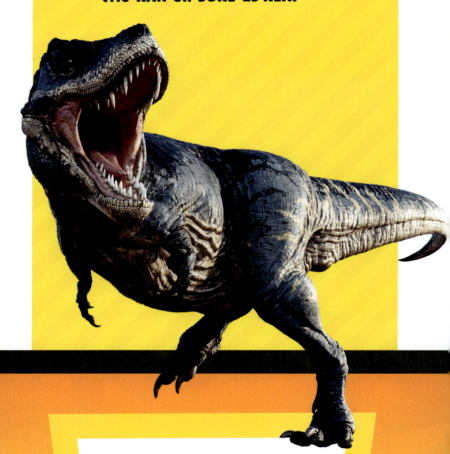

T-Rex lived in what is now western North America.

Its teeth were serrated, or bumpy, like steak knives. Each tooth was up to 12 inches (30.5 centimeters) long.

WOW!

Tyrannosaurus rex had the strongest bite of any land animal that ever lived.

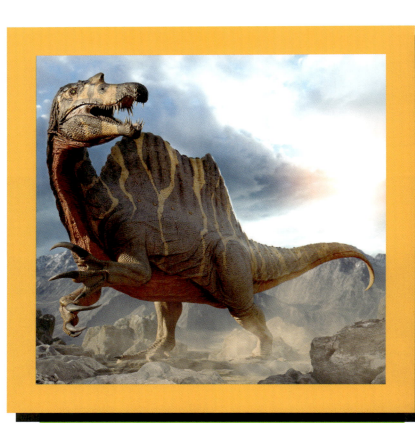

SPINOSAURUS (SPINE-oh-SORE-us)

Spinosaurus had a large sail that stood on its back.

These dinos lived in present-day Egypt and Morocco.

WOW!

A long snout and cone-shaped teeth helped it catch fish to eat.

GALLIMIMUS (GAL-uh-MY-mus)

Gallimimus means "chicken mimic."

They were located in present-day Mongolia.

A full-grown Gallimimus weighed half a ton (454 kg).

ARGENTINOSAURUS
(AR-gen-teen-oh-SORE-us)

Argentinosaurus was 100 feet (30 m) long.

Its thigh bone was just over 8 feet (2.4 m) long.

WOW!

Argentinosaurus is still the largest known dinosaur.

BARYONYX (bah-ree-ON-icks)

Baryonyx was a surf-and-turf eater. It liked steak and seafood.

They lived in present-day England and Spain.

WOW!

Its jaws and teeth looked much like those of today's crocodiles.

SAUROLOPHUS (SORE-oh-LOAF-us)

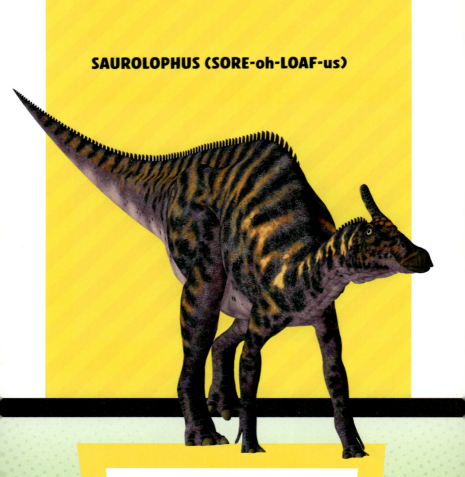

Saurolophus was 27 feet (8.2 m) long.

Most duck-billed dinos could blow air through their crests to make noises, but Saurolophus had a crest made of solid bone.

TSINTAOSAURUS (SIN-tao-SORE-us)

The first Tsintaosaurus fossils included a skull with a spike on its forehead.

NEDOCERATOPS (NED-oh-SER-ah-tops)

Nedoceratops was 23 feet (7 m) long.

Nedoceratops is on its third name. When it was first discovered, it was named Diceratops. Then, scientists thought it was just an unusual Triceratops. Finally, it was given a new name—Nedoceratops.

MONTANACERATOPS (mon-TAN-ah-SER-ah-tops)

They lived in present-day Montana (United States) and Canada.